prophets &
promises

DEVOTIONS FOR
ADVENT & CHRISTMAS
2022–2023

AUGSBURG FORTRESS

Minneapolis

PROPHETS AND PROMISES
Devotions for Advent and Christmas 2022–2023

Scripture quotations are from the New Revised Standard Version Bible, copyright © 1989 by the Division of Christian Education of the National Council of the Churches of Christ in the USA. Used by permission. All rights reserved.

References to ELW are from *Evangelical Lutheran Worship*, copyright © 2006 Evangelical Lutheran Church in America.

"Household blessings and prayers" are from *Bread for the Day 2023: Daily Bible Readings and Prayers* © 2022 Augsburg Fortress.

pISBN 978-1-5064-8802-8
eISBN 978-1-5064-9110-3

Writers: Harvard Stephens Jr. (November 27–December 5), Lydia Posselt (December 6–13), Laura R. Holck (December 14–20), Richard (Dick) Bruesehoff (December 21–29), Troy M. Troftgruben (December 30–January 6)

Editor: Laurie J. Hanson
Cover design: Alisha Lofgren
Cover and interior images: All images © Getty Images. Used by permission.
Interior design and typesetting: Eileen Engebretson

The paper used in this publication meets the minimum requirements of American National Standard for Information Sciences—Permanence of Paper for Printed Library Materials, ANSI Z329.48-1984.

Manufactured in the USA.

23   22   1   2   3   4   5

Welcome

Prophets and Promises continues the Christian tradition of setting aside time to prepare for the celebration of Jesus' birth and to anticipate his return. The Advent season of preparation then unfolds in the joy of the twelve days of Christmas and the day of Epiphany. You will find daily devotions here for the first Sunday of Advent (November 27, 2022) through Epiphany (January 6, 2023). Each devotion features a scripture reading (many from Matthew), accompanied by a photo, a quote to ponder, a reflection, and a prayer. The book also offers household blessings and prayers (see pages 86–94) to enrich your preparations and celebrations.

In ancient times prophets announced God's promises of a deliverer to the Hebrew people. As you read this devotional, look for these ancient promises, even in the Gospel of Matthew. Also watch for the different ways in which Joseph, the magi, and King Herod respond to the arrival of Jesus. Marvel at the power of God's promises, and the mystery of God with us in a newborn child.

May God's lasting promises give you hope, and the good news of Emmanuel's birth fill you with wonder and peace!

November 27 / Advent 1

Isaiah 2:4-5
[The Lord] shall judge between the nations,
and shall arbitrate for many peoples;
they shall beat their swords into plowshares,
and their spears into pruning hooks;
nation shall not lift up sword against nation,
neither shall they learn war any more.
O house of Jacob, come, let us walk
in the light of the Lord!

To ponder
Like the sun, I'm here to shine.
Like the voice, I'm here to sing.

Like the bird, I'm here to fly
and soar high over everything.
—Grace Byers, *I Am Enough*

We are here to shine

Exuberance is a marvelous spiritual gift that inspires in us the cheerfulness and excitement we will need during the weeks of Advent.

The ancient prophets help us encounter the wonders of the living word as their energizing messages announce new things that will soon appear. God often surprises us with the words and actions of people who find unexpected ways to draw us out of darkness and despair. Sometimes we simply marvel when our children, our elders, or friends we haven't seen in years seem to be sent by God to remind us that there is already joy in this world.

Faithful ones, let us give thanks for all those living among us who help refresh our faith in the One who makes all things new. Let us pay attention to the surprising voices around us who speak and live with an exuberance that calls us to believe with all our hearts that we are here to shine.

Prayer

Here I am, Lord. Thank you for all the ways you call me to walk in your light. Amen.

Psalm 122:1-4

I was glad when they said to me,
"Let us go to the house of the LORD."
Now our feet are standing
within your gates, O Jerusalem.
Jerusalem is built as a city
that is at unity with itself;
to which the tribes go up, the tribes of the LORD,
the assembly of Israel, to praise the name of the LORD.

To ponder

We need to have a place that is *here*, connected to these streets, giving a center to this land, welcoming us to our own participation in the integration of human identity with a peaceful place in the natural world. The meeting for church is such a place.—Gordon W. Lathrop, *Holy Things*

The light we share

The ancient Israelites made pilgrimages to Jerusalem's holy temple to worship in God's presence. During the four weeks of Advent we too make a pilgrimage—to the coming of Christ.

Advent candles mark our progress through this time of preparation. We light candles as we ponder the mysteries of the Light of the world. Whether our lives overflow with joy, or we find ourselves struggling with adversity, we believe that the light of Christ has come and still is found among us. It honors and illuminates the sacred spaces that we are blessed to find in our churches, in our communities, in our homes, and especially in our hearts.

Rest your feet and warm your heart in the company of those God sends to be near you. The light we share is a sign of the presence of Christ.

Prayer

Thank you, dear Lord, for the light of your love. Let it shine in our hearts today. Amen.

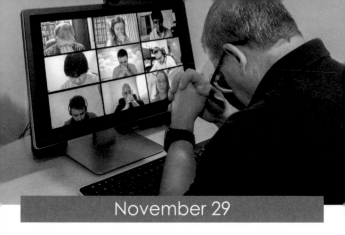

Psalm 122:6-7

Pray for the peace of Jerusalem:
"May they prosper who love you.
Peace be within your walls
and quietness within your towers.
For the sake of my kindred and companions,
I pray for your prosperity.
Because of the house of the LORD our God,
I will seek to do you good."

To ponder

Compassion is the daily practice of recognizing and accepting our shared humanity so that we treat ourselves and others with loving-kindness, and we take action in the face of suffering. . . . Compassion is fueled by understanding and accepting that we're all made of strength and struggle—no one is immune to pain or suffering. Compassion is not a practice of "better than" or "I can fix you"—it's a practice based in the beauty and pain of shared humanity.—Brené Brown, *Atlas of the Heart*

God with us

COVID-19 and its variants have brought pain, suffering, and confusion to our homes and schools, our places of work, and our communities of faith. This public health crisis has not been constrained by the privileges of material wealth; it has become a potent and often unwelcome sign of our shared humanity.

Amid all of this, however, God has given us strength to love and wisdom to act in ways we might never have chosen apart from the suffering we share. We are learning how to reach out to one another—even when social distancing is required. Be encouraged by the mutual care we can give and receive.

The Advent journey continues to call us to pray as we respond to the needs of others. You and I are important signs of God's presence, and nothing we do is too small to embody God's gifts of healing and peace.

Prayer

Lord, be merciful and bless us—that we may be a blessing to others. Amen.

November 30

Romans 13:11-12

You know what time it is, how it is now the moment for you to wake from sleep. For salvation is nearer to us now than when we became believers; the night is far gone, the day is near.

To ponder

We rupture relationships, dishonor the Divine, make unfortunate choices, and try to hide our faults. And yet, Julian (of Norwich) insists, "All will be well and all will be well and every kind of thing shall be well." Take that in. This assertion is meant to penetrate the fog of our despair and wake us up.
—Mirabai Starr, *Forgiving*

When we wake up

When the living word calls us to wake up, we may be surprised to find that in some respects we have indeed been sleeping. Not all slumber is peaceful; not all resting strengthens our faith. Sometimes we have been lulled to sleep by the illusions of a world that makes injustice and poverty and despair appear normal.

But now is the time to wake up! Jesus' redeeming love empowers us to participate in the renewal of all creation. As his grace heals our hearts and minds, we become inspired by new visions of what our life together can be. In ways unique to each of us, we become messengers and heralds who announce the coming of the Lord. Because Jesus is near, we can find new and amazing ways to be near to one another.

This is a season of holy surprises—wake-up calls reminding us that our hearts and hands and voices are needed now, like never before.

Prayer

Holy One, as you come near to us, awaken in us the courage and creativity we need to make known the promises of our faith. Amen.

December 1

Matthew 24:36, 42

"About that day and hour no one knows, neither the angels
of heaven, nor the Son, but only the Father.... Keep awake
therefore, for you do not know on what day your Lord is
coming."

To ponder

God knows you in and out, left and right, through and
through, up and down. God knows you more than you know
yourself. And this God who knows you so well loves you even
more than you can know.—Mary Martha Kannass, sermon,
March 8, 2006

What faith knows

We've all heard the phrase "God only knows." It's a common way to end speculation about things we can neither prove nor predict. And the truth is, God does not disclose everything to us. There are things only God knows.

We do know, however, that God's promises are trustworthy. We can celebrate the promises kept in the life, death, and resurrection of Jesus; rejoice in what God is doing right now; and trust in the promises that God will one day fulfill.

The love of God is made known to us in Jesus. God's love for us, our love for God, and our love for one another are all meant to intertwine and interact. During these weeks in Advent, take time to share God's love with others. Speaking and acting with love are dependable signs that Christ is with us now.

Prayer

God of mystery, thank you for promises fulfilled, promises yet to come, and your love that will not let us go. Amen.

born November
Married at Grand Rapids
December 3ᵈ 1889.
and theyr Childun:

anna born. Oct 30. 1890.
Julius .. Aug 12 1892.
Tibrand .. May 11. 1894.
Jennie .. Aug 30. 1896. died

December 2

Matthew 1:1-2, 5-6

An account of the genealogy of Jesus the Messiah, the son of David, the son of Abraham. Abraham was the father of Isaac, and Isaac the father of Jacob, and Jacob the father of Judah and his brothers, . . . and Boaz the father of Obed by Ruth, and Obed the father of Jesse, and Jesse the father of King David.

To ponder

Cutting off a person from his or her community can have devastating consequences. . . . A person [has] nowhere to go where [they] would be considered a real human being again. . . . Communal acceptance remains one of the gifts congregations can offer people.—Roy Oswald and Arland Jacobson, *The Emotional Intelligence of Jesus*

14

Knowing who we are

Matthew's gospel begins in a unique way, tracing Jesus' ancestry all the way back to Abraham and Sarah. This defiant validation of Jesus' lineage shows God's grace unfolding over many centuries through the people in this family tree.

Today an increasing number of genealogical documents and tools are available to the public. For many Indigenous and displaced groups of people, however, records were not preserved and histories are often distorted or ignored. Helping to uncover details from the past may be helpful, but it is even more important for individuals and congregations to listen to the stories of people who have been marginalized and to honor the truth that these siblings in Christ share.

Prayer

We praise you, God of our ancestors, for your faithfulness to your people in every generation. Empower us to do what is just and to love what is kind as we walk humbly in your name. Amen.

December 3

Matthew 1:6, 16

And David was the father of Solomon by the wife of Uriah, ... and Jacob the father of Joseph the husband of Mary, of whom Jesus was born, who is called the Messiah.

To ponder

Basketball . . . taught [my brother Craig] how to approach strangers when he wanted to snag a spot in a pickup game. He learned . . . a friendly form of . . . trash-talking his bigger, faster opponents on the court. It helped [reinforce] . . . the possibility—something that had long been a credo of my dad's—that most people were good people if you just treated them well. Even the sketchy guys who hung out in front of the corner liquor store lit up when they spotted Craig, calling his name and high-fiving him as we passed by. "How do you even know them?" I'd ask, incredulous. "I don't know. They just know me," he'd say with a shrug. —Michelle Obama, *Becoming*

Grace beyond expectations

Jesus' ancestors were people who often struggled to discover the meaning and purpose of their lives. Somehow as they grew older, their talents and abilities were revealed. Jesus was a carpenter's son. Craig was a gifted athlete. Cousin Robert could really sing. Aunt Shirley learned to speak four languages.

Let the coming of Christ remind us to cherish the good in the human family and in ourselves. Let us find joy in acknowledging and supporting people of all ages and circumstances who need to be known and appreciated for who they are. We all come from somewhere, and by the grace of God, we are all becoming something more than this world might expect us to be. Never forget that, even if we don't know them, people may know about us. Can't that be a good thing?

Prayer

Gracious God, we thank you for all the ways you lead and guide us along the paths of life. Bless all those you send to support and care for us. Thank you for those you have placed in our care. Amen.

December 4 / Advent 2

Isaiah 11:1-2
A shoot shall come out from the stump of Jesse,
and a branch shall grow out of his roots.
The spirit of the Lord shall rest on him,
the spirit of wisdom and understanding,
the spirit of counsel and might,
the spirit of knowledge and the fear of the Lord.

To ponder
When you open the doors
To a shelter,
After a bad storm has passed,
Ain't that air sweet? Even if the

Town is in splinters? Ain't
You happy that storm tried its level best
But couldn't stop your heart?
—Cornelius Eady, "We as People"

Come, Holy Spirit

David, Jesse's youngest son, was a great king, but later in ancient Israel's history the kingdom was split in two, conflicts developed with neighboring kingdoms, and the people suffered. Dreams of restoration seemed foolish. We may not expect much from an old tree stump, but the prophet Isaiah is in awe of signs of life among people who seem to have lost everything. That is why he celebrates the power of the Holy Spirit resting on a new branch.

Could we be part of this new branch? Look for the spiritual gifts listed by Isaiah. Where do these gifts appear in our lives, in our communities, amid the struggles and storms of our times? Where is God doing something new and wonderful—right now?

Just as ancient trees rejoice when tender saplings appear, people of God find hope in the stories of families and communities who can tell the world that when they were down to nothing, God was up to something!

Prayer

Spirit of the living God, fall fresh on me. Amen.

Isaiah 11:6-7, 10

The wolf shall live with the lamb,
the leopard shall lie down with the kid,
the calf and the lion and the fatling together,
and a little child shall lead them.
The cow and the bear shall graze,
their young shall lie down together;
and the lion shall eat straw like the ox. . . .
On that day the root of Jesse shall stand as a signal to the
peoples.

To ponder

[The wolf cub] often tried to get the dogs to come play with
him, but they invariably ignored him. But on this day they

came without being invited, all of them. . . . Now the lonely wolf was part of a happy family. He smelled them, kissed them, and licked them all over and over. A happier wolf, Chen Zhen thought, would be hard to find.—Jiang Rong, *Wolf Totem*

A new way to live

Today God's promise of peace and hope expands with images of wild animals no longer depicted as lethal adversaries. Fearsome creatures have become playful friends. It almost seems as if the prophet has drafted a story for children that is perfectly suited for this season—and there's nothing wrong with that.

How can we become like wolves and calves, leopards and lambs—no longer living as enemies, but working together to care for the most vulnerable among us? The Holy Spirit moves us to faithfully imagine and celebrate the wonderful signs of a world made new. The nations may wonder why we sing our hymns, tell our ancient stories, and adorn our Christmas trees with symbols of a world reconciled in joy and peace, but we tell all who will listen that God is calling all of us to learn a new way to live.

Prayer

Faithful God, empower us to tell the sacred stories of a world made new through the coming of Christ. Amen.

December 6

Psalm 72:1, 6-7

Give the king your justice, O God,
and your righteousness to the king's son; . . .
Let him come down like rain upon the mown field,
like showers that water the earth . . .
and let there be an abundance of peace
till the moon shall be no more.

To ponder

The way I see it, there is no "head of the table" in [God's]
queendom; the table is round.—Kyndall Rae Rathaus, *Thy
Queendom Come*

A place for everyone

Jesus' story does not fit the usual narrative of a king. His birth was celebrated by shepherds, and his first crib was an animal feeding trough. He did not organize a coup, storm the castle, and establish himself as a new—and much kinder—king. Instead he got right to work, leveling the playing field, giving up all the power and privilege that was due to him as the Son of God, king of the universe. His conquering campaign involved teaching, feeding, and hanging out with people who were sick and those who were homeless. He was crowned with thorns, and his coronation ceremony was his torture and death. His throne was a cross.

In this new kind of kingdom and with a different kind of power, Jesus builds new families and bigger tables, so that everyone has a place—including you.

Prayer

Lord Jesus, remind me that your true power lies in love, humility, and justice. Amen.

Romans 15:4-6

Whatever was written in former days was written for our instruction, so that by steadfastness and by the encouragement of the scriptures we might have hope. May the God of steadfastness and encouragement grant you to live in harmony with one another, in accordance with Christ Jesus, so that together you may with one voice glorify the God and Father of our Lord Jesus Christ.

To ponder

For better or for worse, there are seasons when we hold our faith, and then there are seasons when our faith holds us.
—Rachel Held Evans and Jeff Chu, *Wholehearted Faith*

Instructions for the best Advent

Many years ago, I was a college student at home for Christmas break. I insisted on decorating the Christmas tree, even though my mom was less than enthusiastic about it. When I left to go back to college for the January term, guess who was left to take down the tree? The following year, I believe we set up the pre-lit tree and didn't even get around to putting on ornaments.

In the last few years, I've been motivated to start strong every Advent, to read daily devotions and take time to reflect on the season. Then, after a week or two, I realize I have done almost none of the things I intended to do.

Thankfully, God is faithful, whether we check off everything on our Advent to-do lists—or nothing at all. We don't know exactly where this Advent and Christmas will take us, but we do know where God will be. God is right here, in the beginnings and the endings, in the starting strong and in the fizzling out, in the dying and in the rising.

Prayer

Guide, encourage, and strengthen me in my flagging steps, Lord Jesus. Amen.

December 8

Romans 15:7

Welcome one another, therefore, just as Christ has welcomed you, for the glory of God.

To ponder

A story can happen inside us . . . some part of you might die and a new self will rise up to take its place.—Sue Monk Kidd, *The Book of Longings*

Making room for Jesus

Have you ever had one of those "airplane" moments? You happen to be sitting next to someone on an airplane, you exchange pleasantries, since you both have the same destination . . . and suddenly you are trading pictures of pets and grandkids, sharing with each other your deepest hurts and wildest dreams. Next you have a standing Thanksgiving invitation or you are making plans to attend their PhD dissertation-defense party.

We welcome one another when we create space for each other—for all our stories and all our experiences. We do this not because these people *might* be Jesus, but because they *are* Jesus. When we see Jesus in one another, we make space, we invite, we welcome, we reach out, and we go out of our way.

That's all we need to do, really, to follow and imitate Jesus. Be the church, not "go to church." Create relationships, not programs. Build up the body of Christ, not buildings. Open not just our doors, but our hearts as well.

Prayer

Spirit of the living God, enfold us and surround us with your welcome, and inspire us to show radical welcome to others. Amen.

December 9

Matthew 3:1-2, 5-6

In those days John the Baptist appeared in the wilderness of Judea, proclaiming, "Repent, for the kingdom of heaven has come near." . . . Then the people of Jerusalem and all Judea were going out to him, and all the region along the Jordan, and they were baptized by him in the river Jordan, confessing their sins.

To ponder

Though we are not fully free and the dream not fully realized, yet, we are not what we used to be and not what we will be.
—James H. Cone, *The Cross and the Lynching Tree*

Inflatable John the Baptist

By this time in Advent you may be seeing manger scenes in church foyers, on holiday cards, and lit up in front of homes. Meanwhile, Mary, Joseph, shepherds, and baby Jesus are noticeably absent from our Advent readings. Instead, we have . . . John the Baptist!

In the first church I served, my copastor joked about his neighbor's yard, which was full of inflatable winter scenes and cartoon characters, but no John the Baptist. He would spend every Advent wondering, with a smile, why John wasn't part of every outdoor nativity set, especially since the baptizer is a good candidate to be a big, loud, slightly scary lit-up figure that startles passersby.

Well, why not a giant, light-up John the Baptist? After all, John's message is the same as the message of Advent: The kingdom of God is coming near. God's arrival is just around the corner.

Prayer

Transforming God, the world around me wants to skip to a happy ending, but help me to see, hear, and wait for your arrival. Amen.

December 10

Matthew 3:7-8, 11

When [John] saw many Pharisees and Sadducees coming for baptism, he said to them, "You brood of vipers! Who warned you to flee from the wrath to come? Bear fruit worthy of repentance. . . . I baptize you with water for repentance, but one who is more powerful than I is coming after me; I am not worthy to carry his sandals. He will baptize you with the Holy Spirit and fire."

To ponder

We recognize that even Jesus was fully human, given to despair and anger . . . but we fail to extend the same grace to ourselves.
—Emmy Kegler, *For All Who Are Weary*

People, get ready

John the Baptist's surprising words to the Pharisees and Sadducees are not exactly ones you will find on a festive holiday card. After all, this is supposed to be a time of joy and peace and a silent night!

But December is not joyful and peaceful for everyone. We miss loved ones who can't be with us and those who have died. Families struggle to get along. Drivers on the road are impatient. Shopkeepers and sales staff are worn out from crabby customers and long hours. Nations are embroiled in conflicts. Hunger, poverty, homelessness, oppression, and greed continue.

All was not joyful and peaceful when Jesus was born, either. The land was occupied by Rome. Most people struggled just to survive. The baby Jesus cried, as all infants do. He grew up, stubbed his toe, fed those who were hungry, and healed those who were sick. He was angry about the injustices people faced—and continue to face.

John the Baptist points to Jesus and tells us to get ready for his coming. Jesus then points us to the way of the Lord, the way of the waters of repentance and cleansing and rebirth. This may not be the way we would expect, but it's the one we and the world need.

Prayer

Gracious God, pour out your Spirit so that I may be forgiven, refreshed, and renewed. Amen.

December 11 / Advent 3

Isaiah 35:1
The wilderness and the dry land shall be glad,
the desert shall rejoice and blossom;
like the crocus it shall blossom abundantly,
and rejoice with joy and singing.

To ponder
To be a hill, to be a sandy beach, to be a Saturday, all are possible verbs in a world where everything is alive.—Robin Wall Kimmerer, *Braiding Sweetgrass*

To be a nut

One thousand people from around the world arrived in Windhoek, Namibia, in May 2017 for the Twelfth Assembly of the Lutheran World Federation. Although the country's name comes from the Namib desert, makalani trees and their nuts are plentiful. Each participant in the celebration received a makalani nut that a local artisan had hand-carved with the assembly theme. In the cool of the morning and evening, participants worshiped together under a huge tent among trees growing in the hotel parking lot. What an unlikely sight—trees in the middle of a parking lot, in the middle of a desert country, were suddenly in the middle of one thousand Lutherans!

A nut is a seed that lies in wait for water, ready for new life, ready to grow into something beautiful and powerful, like a makalani tree. God's sustaining spirit drowns our fear and makes our desert hearts bloom. We grow into something beautiful and powerful so that we can bear fruit—fruit that is not ours to keep but to give away.

Prayer

Living God, bring me hope in parched times, and joy in abundant times. Amen.

December 12

Isaiah 35:6-7

For waters shall break forth in the wilderness,
and streams in the desert;
the burning sand shall become a pool,
and the thirsty ground springs of water;
the haunt of jackals shall become a swamp,
the grass shall become reeds and rushes.

To ponder

God of loneliness and longing, of bushfires and wilderness,
of soup kitchens and border towns, of snowfall and children,
teach us to love the world again.—Sarah Bessey, *A Rhythm
of Prayer*

On the edge

I am stuck in a wilderness: I'm lost and I stumble, and I tend to go in circles. I am woefully unprepared. While there are no wild animals, quicksand, or dangerous terrain here, plenty of pitfalls and traps await: bills, frayed relationships, an unforeseen diagnosis. Physical, mental, and emotional wilderness persists. In the wilderness I am at the mercy of forces I can't predict or control.

The Bible tells of wildernesses and wilderness experiences. Hagar, Moses, John the Baptist, Jesus, and many more found life here, because wildernesses are not just places of danger, they are places on the edge, places of renewal—places where old patterns are obliterated and new patterns take hold and flourish. The old haunt of our jackal thoughts becomes a safe place, lush and life-giving. The sand that burned us with shame is transformed into a baptismal pool of promised new life.

Prayer

Though I feel lost, O Lord, I know you are with me. Create in me new channels of life. Amen.

December 13

Isaiah 35:8, 10

A highway shall be there,
and it shall be called the Holy Way; . . .
no traveler, not even fools, shall go astray. . . .
And the ransomed of the LORD shall return,
and come to Zion with singing;
everlasting joy shall be upon their heads;
they shall obtain joy and gladness,
and sorrow and sighing shall flee away.

To ponder

Hopefully, by the end of our journey, we will achieve something we never dreamed of when we took that first step. We will have become heroes, albeit unsung and unseen by most folk.—Mital Perkins, *Steeped in Stories*

Highway to health

Here on God's highway there is good news. Sinners are welcomed. The poor are fed. The broken are healed and made whole again. Streams run where there once was barren desert. On this highway even we fools will not get lost along the way. There are cracks of hope in the stone that seals our tombs, a light shines through, and what we believed was as good as dead refuses to stay that way.

I believe that God has been faithful to foolish little me over and over again in the journey that has brought me to this time and this place. It has not always been smooth going, but God has proven to me that great things happen according to God's promises. God always goes beyond my hopes and expectations.

Prayer

Even when my feet are heavy and I trip over my own good intentions, Lord Jesus, guide my steps and lead my way. Amen.

Psalm 146:5-6

Happy are they who have
the God of Jacob for their help,
whose hope is in the Lord their God;
who made heaven and earth, the seas,
and all that is in them;
who keeps promises forever.

To ponder

[Jesus said to the disciples,] "You did not choose me but I
chose you. And I appointed you to go and bear fruit, fruit that
will last."—John 15:16

Choose me

Jacob was the second-born twin who cheated his brother Esau out of his inheritance and his birthright. Esau flies into a murderous rage and vows to kill his brother. We might expect Esau's righteous vindication as the next scene. But scripture tells us little about Esau. The story instead follows Jacob, the cheat and liar who has done wrong.

We witness Jacob's most intimate and vulnerable moments: his flight into the desert, his dream of angels going up and down on a ladder to heaven as he tosses and turns in the sand, and his first meeting with the girl he loves. Through it all Jacob's character continues to be less than stellar. He ends up with four wives, cheats his father-in-law out of his flocks, and uses his entire family as a physical buffer between himself and Esau when they finally reunite.

But God, who made all things and keeps promises forever, keeps choosing Jacob and never stops, no matter what. God had promised that Jacob's children would become as numerous as the grains of sand he had lain in, and that they would spread in all directions. God keeps choosing Jacob because God intends to keep that promise, no matter what Jacob does.

Jacob's God is also ours. Happy are we when we choose the One who never stops choosing us.

Prayer

God of promises, help us turn to you as you keep choosing us. Amen.

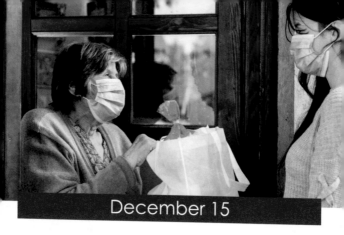

December 15

Psalm 146:8-9

The LORD opens the eyes of the blind;
the LORD lifts up those who are bowed down;
the LORD loves the righteous.
The LORD cares for the stranger;
the LORD sustains the orphan and widow,
but frustrates the way of the wicked.

To ponder

Dear Church, we have to wage peace in the name of Jesus
Christ for this generation. We have to break the chains of
sin and death holding all of us captive.—Lenny Duncan,
Dear Church

Do what the Lord does

If you want to hear about the power of God, read the psalms. God creates and destroys, raises up kings and prophets, heals and knows. God hears us, answers us, celebrates with us, and comforts us.

What we may forget amid the grandeur and spectacle of the psalms is that God is an incarnated, "in the flesh" God, not a mystical, all-powerful puppet master orchestrating things just off stage. Although prayers are needed, it is not enough for us to pray and wait for God to change the world. *God works in and through people.* Our actions must follow our prayers, because through us God intends to change the world, to bring about a community of love and peace for all people.

In partnership with God, we are called to do small things that change our immediate world. Sometimes these things remain small and sometimes they gain momentum and become much larger than us, but we are not to concern ourselves with the outcome. We are called simply to do, relying on the God of incarnation to strengthen us and to fuel larger change for the good of all.

Prayer

Give us vision and strength, all-powerful God, to love our neighbors and change our world. Amen.

December 16

James 5:7-8, 10

Be patient, therefore, beloved, until the coming of the Lord. The farmer waits for the precious crop from the earth, being patient with it until it receives the early and the late rains. You also must be patient. Strengthen your hearts, for the coming of the Lord is near. . . . As an example of suffering and patience, beloved, take the prophets who spoke in the name of the Lord.

To ponder

But farmers are patient [people] tried by brutal seasons, and if they weren't plagued by dreams of generation, few would keep plowing, spring after spring.—Richard Powers, *The Overstory*

An act of faith

People who work the land know how to make crops grow, but the outcome of their work is dependent upon more than their plowing, sowing, and fertilizing. Their "dreams of generation" and the efforts of their days are also subject to larger forces of nature: wind, drought, rain, deluge, early frost, scorching heat, insects, fungus, disease. They teach us that patience has something to do with steady work in the face of the unknown, trust in the goodness of life itself, and gentle persistence as things unfold in time. Farming is an act of faith.

The prophets too know something about this kind of waiting, perhaps to an even greater extreme than farmers. They work and speak, suffer and love, standing their ground in the presence of threat and active resistance. Prophesying is an act of faith.

Patience is not just waiting for the passing of time; patience is the persistence of character and commitment in anticipation of the goodness for which we are giving our moments and our days. James asks us to strengthen our hearts in the knowledge that we wait for the One who called and named us, the One who has given us good work, and the One who keeps promises. Advent waiting is an act of faith.

Prayer

Find us, O God, in our waiting places and reward our patience with strength. Amen.

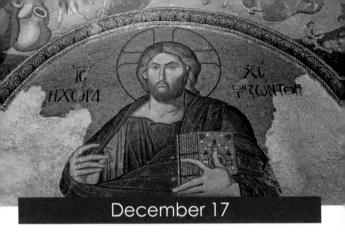

Matthew 11:2-5

When John heard in prison what the Messiah was doing, he sent word by his disciples and said to him, "Are you the one who is to come, or are we to wait for another?" Jesus answered them, "Go and tell John what you hear and see: the blind receive their sight, the lame walk, the lepers are cleansed, the deaf hear, the dead are raised, and the poor have good news brought to them."

To ponder

Gods always behave like the people who make them.—Zora Neale Hurston, *Tell My Horse*

Who are you?

From the moment he was conceived, John was meant to prepare the way for the Messiah. His was a life of simplicity in the wilderness, a life of proclamation and preparation. John even baptized people for the repentance of their sins. So why doesn't he recognize the Messiah? And here's a scarier thought: If the one who has been preparing for the Messiah his whole life doesn't recognize him, what chance do we have?

Jesus wasn't quite what John expected. From his jail cell John sends his followers to ask, "Are you the one?" Jesus doesn't answer the question. He simply tells John's disciples to report that they see the words of the prophet Isaiah being fulfilled: people receive healing, good news is preached, the dead live.

We, like John, are preparing our hearts to receive a Messiah we have underestimated, miscalculated, and misunderstood. We are asked to prepare our hearts for a Savior we do not completely know and won't completely recognize. We are asked to prepare our hearts for the One who fulfills the words of the prophets; One who keeps the law; One who embodies wisdom even and especially if that will shock us.

We are asked to prepare for a Messiah who exceeds our expectations and challenges the limitations we put on grace.

Prayer

Awaken us from the prisons of our own making, O God, and shock us with your power and goodness. Amen.

December 18 / Advent 4

Isaiah 7:10, 14

The LORD spoke to Ahaz, saying, . . . "the Lord himself will give you a sign. Look, the young woman is with child and shall bear a son, and shall name him Immanuel."

To ponder

I need a God who is with us always, everywhere, in the deepest depths as well as the highest heights.—Madeleine L'Engle, *Two-Part Invention*

Show us a sign

Signs serve one of four purposes: *direction*, pointing to destinations; *safety*, teaching rules and warning of potential dangers;

information, posting instructions; and *identification*, labeling where things are.

Signs are meant for strangers. When we know a place, we stop looking at signs. They move into the background and we begin to navigate subconsciously. Nothing makes this phenomenon more obvious than when a new traffic sign is installed in the neighborhood. The tendency to not see what is now there means new traffic lights must blink for a period of days before beginning operation. New stop signs must be new labeled "new" so residents are jolted off autopilot and into a new reality.

In Ahaz's day, things were changing. God promised a sign, a kind of new blinking traffic light for all to see. A young woman would have a child called "Immanuel," marking a transformational shift. God, it seems, would be with the people forevermore. Can you imagine Ahaz's response? He must have developed a heightened awareness as he began to anticipate the coming and nearness of God.

Can we anticipate God in the same way? Can we look for clues in the changes around us, both large and small? Perhaps God is making a way and creating a home in the things that seem unfamiliar to us. There are new signs all around us. They have the potential to change us, just as they must have changed Ahaz.

Prayer

From your nearness, O God, show us a sign. Amen.

December 19

Psalm 80:1-3

Hear, O Shepherd of Israel, leading Joseph like a flock;
shine forth, you that are enthroned upon the cherubim.
In the presence of Ephraim, Benjamin, and Manasseh,
stir up your strength and come to help us.
Restore us, O God; let your face shine upon us,
and we shall be saved.

To ponder

Lighthouses don't go running all over an island looking for
boats to save; they just stand there shining.—Anne Lamott,
Bird by Bird

Already at work

When we are in trouble, our need of God, our lack, and our desires become crystal clear. Our prayers become both focused and fervent, our anticipation of God's intervention heightened. We begin to pray as if God is aloof and inactive, or completely unaware of our circumstances, as if God needs to be awakened to our cause. We forget that God is Emmanuel, always with us and always *in it* with us.

God's light is already shining on our weary world, pointing the way, bringing hope and healing, causing peace. But sometimes we are weak, suffering, despairing. Prolonged difficulties make holding onto faith a challenge. But that's actually what faith is: believing in spite of the current evidence, holding fast to a promise when there's no indication it will ever be fulfilled.

Faith may not change our circumstances, but it can change our perspective, and it can change our prayers. Faith can cause us to cry out to God, knowing that God already sees, already knows, and is already at work. Faith can help us look to God instead of ourselves, to develop patience, and to hope with expectation.

Prayer

O God, help us see your light, already shining. Amen.

December 20

Romans 1:1-5

Paul, a servant of Jesus Christ, called to be an apostle, set apart for the gospel of God, which he promised beforehand through his prophets in the holy scriptures, the gospel concerning his Son, who was descended from David according to the flesh and was declared to be Son of God with power according to the spirit of holiness by resurrection from the dead, Jesus Christ our Lord, through whom we have received grace and apostleship to bring about the obedience of faith among all the Gentiles for the sake of his name.

To ponder

Introduce yourself. Be accountable as the one who comes asking for life.—Robin Wall Kimmerer, *Braiding Sweetgrass*

What's in an introduction?

There were many ways Paul could have introduced himself. He was a tent maker, an expert in the law, a resident of Jerusalem, a devout Jew. He could have introduced himself from his own notoriety. He could have introduced himself through his connections. He could have solicited a recommendation from someone the Romans already respected.

But he doesn't do any of that. Paul introduces himself by saying he is a servant of Jesus; called to be an apostle; consecrated for the good news of God and the spread of its reach to the ends of the earth.

There is at the same time a humility and a power in Paul's introduction. He is just one person playing a role in a divine action. He is saying he's willing to do whatever it takes, whatever Jesus asks, for faithfulness in the God of life to flourish on the earth. He comes simply endorsed by Jesus.

Think about all the introductions we hear and the ones we use ourselves. Are they full of credentials? Name-dropping hoping for "an in"? Leaning on other people's reputations or our own? How would our lives shift if we began introducing ourselves as people serving the Source of life? As people asking for life? As people searching everywhere for life?

Prayer

Teach us to be your servants first and foremost, O God of Life. Amen.

December 21

Matthew 1:18-19

Now the birth of Jesus the Messiah took place in this way.
When his mother Mary had been engaged to Joseph, but
before they lived together, she was found to be with child from
the Holy Spirit. Her husband Joseph, being a righteous man
and unwilling to expose her to public disgrace, planned to
dismiss her quietly.

To ponder

[Mary] was simply to remain in the world, to go forward
with her marriage to Joseph, to live the life of an artisan's
wife, just what she had planned to do when she had no idea
that anything out of the ordinary would ever happen to her.
It almost seemed as if God's becoming [human] and being

born of a woman were ordinary. . . . God did mean it to be the ordinary thing, for it is [God's] will that Christ shall be born in every human being's life . . . through the ordinary daily life and the human love that people give to one another.—Caryll Houselander, *The Reed of God*

God in a body

We live in bodies. From conception to death, in bodies. Fleshy bodies. Real bodies. Frail, vulnerable bodies. Living, breathing bodies. For all the variety of sizes and ages, genders and skin tones—ordinary bodies. Of course, it's all quite ordinary.

But God in flesh? In a body? Incarnate (which really means "in flesh, in a body")? Inconceivable! Unheard of! Yet here *is* God! Jesus, incarnate, in a body. Mary, his mother, in a body. This is how the birth of Jesus the Messiah takes place. It seems as if it were quite ordinary.

God, creator, kneeling in the dust, blowing life into bodies. Bodies, enslaved in Egypt, liberated. Bodies, wandering in wild lands, brought home. Bodies, wracked with illness, healed. Bodies, torn and tortured by things beyond their control, mended. Bodies, separated, excluded, isolated, restored to community. Quite ordinary.

God's love of us, it seems, is quite ordinary.

Prayer

Living God, be born in us and restore us to life. Amen.

December 22

Matthew 1:20-21

Just when he had resolved to do this, an angel of the Lord appeared to him in a dream and said, "Joseph, son of David, do not be afraid to take Mary as your wife, for the child conceived in her is from the Holy Spirit. She will bear a son, and you are to name him Jesus, for he will save his people from their sins."

To ponder

The remedy for fear is trust in God.—Caryll Houselander, *The Reed of God*

Don't be afraid!

Don't be afraid? You've got to be kidding! The young couple, unmarried, unexpectedly pregnant, faces disgrace and shame. That's a lot to fear. This could cost them a place in their community. It could even cost Mary her life. Hoping to spare her life, and to spare them both from shame, Joseph plans to divorce her quietly. But God intends something quite different. God's work, after all, is saving work. God is giving birth to a community where shame and death threats don't have the last word.

The young couple responds with courage. Joseph does as he was invited, wedding Mary. Mary gives birth to a son named Jesus. God's saving intention becomes real, tangible, embodied in a child—Jesus, whose name means "God saves; God is restoring us."

The story continues to unfold. Shame and guilt lurk in the corners. Death threats persist, first against Jesus the baby, then against Jesus the teacher and healer, finally against his gathered community. But the word still resounds: "Don't be afraid!"

The courage of a young couple to trust the voice of an angel messenger becomes the courage of a community to renounce shame and threats, a community that lives a story of God's saving, restoring work.

Prayer

Jesus, child of the saving God, we yearn for your life-giving word, "Don't be afraid." Amen.

Matthew 1:22-23

All this took place to fulfill what had been spoken by the Lord
through the prophet:
"Look, the virgin shall conceive and bear a son,
and they shall name him Emmanuel,"
which means, "God is with us."

To ponder

All being itself is derived from God and the presence of the
Creator is in each created thing.— Rabbi Menachem Nahum
of Chernobyl, *Upright Practices*

Even here?

It's quite easy to accept the Emmanuel promise—that God is with us—in our imaginations. We can accept the presence of Christ in imaginary people, in people whom we do not know.

It's quite easy to reject the Emmanuel promise that God is with us in the case of our own relatives, in the people we live and work with, in our own neighborhoods, as citizens of a particular nation.

And perhaps it's easiest of all to dismiss the Emmanuel promise when I think of myself. God loves *me*? God dwells in *me*? How can this be?

And right here, torn between accepting and rejecting the Emmanuel promise, is where we live every day. And right here, right now, the promise persists: They shall name him Emmanuel, which means "God is with us"—no ifs, ands, or buts; no conditions; no exceptions.

God speaks the name and it is so: Emmanuel. God is with us.

Prayer

Even here, even now, come quickly, Emmanuel. Amen.

December 24 / Christmas Eve

Matthew 1:24-25

When Joseph awoke from sleep, he did as the angel of the Lord commanded him; he took [Mary] as his wife, but had no marital relations with her until she had borne a son; and he named him Jesus.

To ponder

In our era, the road to holiness necessarily passes through the world of action.—Dag Hammarskjöld, *Markings*

Lights! Camera! Action!

Often when we read something, we look mostly at the nouns, the who and where. Have you ever tried reading something paying special attention to the verbs, the action words? Look again at Matthew's text and notice what's going on.

Joseph *awoke* from his sleep. He recognized that the time for sleeping was past and the time for action was at hand.

Joseph *did* what the angel commanded. There was no need to hesitate or procrastinate. There were no second thoughts. He acted.

Joseph *took* her as his wife. Another translation says, "He took her to his house," where together Joseph and Mary dealt with whatever opposition they faced from family and neighbors and even from a tyrant king. Joseph joined Mary in the risk she was taking.

Joseph *had* no marital relations with Mary. He set himself and his needs aside. For Mary's sake? For the infant's sake? For the Spirit's sake? For our sake?

Joseph *named* him Jesus. To this point in Matthew, all the announcing, the proclaiming has been the voice of an angel. Joseph's is the first human voice to speak the name of Jesus.

The story, the drama, the action has begun.

Prayer

Restoring God, stir us from fear, from lethargy, from complacency to action. Amen.

December 25 / Christmas Day

Isaiah 9:6

For a child has been born for us, a son given to us;
authority rests upon his shoulders;
and he is named Wonderful Counselor, Mighty God,
Everlasting Father, Prince of Peace.

To ponder

Just as the Christ child was born not merely to a human
mother but into a human family, *the* human family, so we too
are part of the Holy Kinship.—Margaret Guenther, *Toward
Holy Ground*

An unbreakable bond

You've probably heard someone say of a newborn baby, "Oh, she looks just like her mother" or "Wow, he's the spitting image of his grandpa." Generation after generation, family resemblance is passed along as a legacy.

Can you imagine a family resemblance, a holy kinship that flows without restriction—from parent to child, from child to parent, between friends and neighbors, between enemies—in every conceivable direction? Can you imagine likeness that moves sideways *between* families, between those who share a far broader bloodline, those who come from a far deeper genetic pool? Can you imagine a holy kinship that unites every person, every bird, every animal, every tree, every stone—in short, all of creation across all time?

Hear the joy-filled word: a child is born for us, Emmanuel, God is with us! We are kin with this child because this child, named Prince of Peace, is kin with us. We have shared a kinship with this child since the beginning of time. Not even death can tear us away from him.

Prayer

You are born for us, Holy One, and you are always with us. Let heaven and nature sing! Amen.

December 26

Isaiah 9:7

His authority shall grow continually,
and there shall be endless peace
for the throne of David and his kingdom.
He will establish and uphold it
with justice and with righteousness
from this time onward and forevermore.
The zeal of the LORD of hosts will do this.

To ponder

My greatest fear is that shalom [peace] will be sold as a local
anesthetic, numbing us in happy tranquility, causing us to
forget the nagging issues of poverty, hunger, oppression, and
racism.—John and Mary Schramm, *Things That Make for Peace*

The work of peace

Can you feel it? Isaiah's promise of endless peace pulses with energy! It is the work, the activity of God's own hands. It is the work of God's justice and righteousness, accomplished before our very eyes. It is renewal and reversal. It's work that may even make our blood boil as it invites and engages us.

Can you hear it? Endless peace is God's own eagerness for a world of justice and righteousness. It's God's passion for a world in which everyone and everything belongs. No one and no thing dismissed or excluded. In fact, this peace is complete only when everyone and everything are included. All find their places. It is a world made whole again, a world throbbing with life, whose heart echoes the beating of God's heart.

Can you see it? God's own yearning for endless peace is embodied, alive, made flesh in Jesus. God's passion is come to life. The zeal of the Lord of hosts is doing this.

Prayer

O God, may our cries and yearnings for peace join us to your passion and your work for endless peace. Amen.

December 27

Psalm 96:1-3
Sing to the LORD a new song;
sing to the LORD, all the earth.
Sing to the LORD, bless the name of the LORD;
proclaim God's salvation from day to day.
Declare God's glory among the nations
and God's wonders among all peoples.

To ponder
Every Who down in Who-ville, the tall and the small,
Was singing! without any presents at all!
—Theodore Seuss Geisel, *How the Grinch Stole Christmas*

Oh, the singing!

Dr. Seuss's classic Christmas book for children of all ages invites us to stand in wordless, holy wonder. What will the Whos do if all the decorations disappear? If the presents aren't presented? If the feasting falters for lack of food?

They'll sing of course! And they'll be in good company.

People once enslaved in Egypt, crossing the Red Sea, sang. Exiles in Babylon, longing for home, sang. Hannah, Elizabeth, and Mary, hearing the promise of a child, sang. Angels, making a birth announcement to shepherds, sang. Early Christians, gathered for worship, sang. They sang, knowing who was making the promises. They knew who they could trust. Oh, the singing!

All of us cling to the same hope. When we're feasting on God's promises, that's enough! We are enough. We have enough. And that's enough. Oh, the singing!

Prayer

Leaning, leaning, safe and secure from all alarms; leaning, leaning, leaning on the everlasting arms. Amen. ("What a fellowship, what a joy divine," ELW 774)

December 28

Psalm 96:11-13

Let the heavens rejoice, and let the earth be glad;
let the sea thunder and all that is in it;
let the field be joyful, and all that is therein.
Then shall all the trees of the wood
shout for joy at your coming, O Lord,
for you come to judge the earth.
You will judge the world with righteousness
and the peoples with your truth.

To ponder

Then let there be rejoicing.—Jan Richardson, *Circle of Grace:
A Book of Blessings for the Seasons*

Cause for rejoicing

Many of us are probably more familiar with a Santa Claus-God than a Christmas-God. Santa is watching! Who's naughty? Don't pout or cry. Have you been good enough? Decidedly childish thoughts and fears, often planted by well-intentioned folks, but the thoughts, the fears, have stuck like burrs. We know the truth about ourselves all too well. We know our failings, our weaknesses, our vulnerabilities. We're too well acquainted with this exacting judge. This righteousness cuts too close to the bone. Never good enough. Never done enough. Not much to be glad about. Little cause for rejoicing.

Not so with this Christmas-God! Can we ever hear it often enough? In love, Christmas-God has come to us. Emmanuel, God-with-us. One with us. One of us. Like a vine and its branches. Never alone. Never abandoned. Never separated.

Can you see it? Are you hearing it? The heavens are kicking up their heels and the earth joins the dancing. The seas leap with joy and the sea monsters are playing along. The fields and pastures clap their hands and the critters hoot and holler. The forests break into song and the birds provide the harmony.

All is well. Don't be afraid. Let there be rejoicing!

Prayer

Holy Child, with all of creation we rejoice that you have come to be with us! Amen.

Titus 3:4-7

When the goodness and loving kindness of God our Savior appeared, he saved us, not because of any works of righteousness that we had done, but according to his mercy, through the water of rebirth and renewal by the Holy Spirit. This Spirit he poured out on us richly through Jesus Christ our Savior, so that, having been justified by his grace, we might become heirs according to the hope of eternal life.

To ponder

To be saved is to be made whole, to be able to enter the unity that lies beyond all of life's contradictions.—Parker Palmer, *The Promise of Paradox*

You belong!

God goes to great lengths to say it, to show it, to demonstrate it, to make it clear: You belong!

Our Advent waiting, our Christmas celebration, and the Epiphany revelation all point in the same direction: God has come down to us. Jesus the Christ is God with us. It's been God's plan since the beginning of time. You belong.

In the face of every voice that disputes, questions, or denies it, a simple, powerful word replies, "You belong."

But the God of promise ramps it up a couple more notches: Not only do you belong, you are named an heir, entitling you to renewed life. The gifts of belonging, of being connected by rebirth are yours. You are whole. You lack nothing.

So, now what? What would your life be like if you trusted this promise? How would you live if you acted as if this were true for you? This is not a game of pretend or wishful thinking. It's a life of clinging to God, holding on to this promise, of embracing and being embraced by Emmanuel, God with us.

Prayer

Emmanuel, God with us, hold us in your loving embrace. Amen.

December 30

Matthew 2:1-2

In the time of King Herod, after Jesus was born in Bethlehem of Judea, wise men from the East came to Jerusalem, asking, "Where is the child who has been born king of the Jews? For we observed his star at its rising, and have come to pay him homage."

To ponder

We must be ready to allow ourselves to be interrupted by God, who will thwart our plans and frustrate our ways time and again, even daily, by sending people across our path. . . . We do not manage our time ourselves but allow it to be occupied by God.—Dietrich Bonhoeffer, *Life Together*

Mysterious messengers

No one knows who the magi were. Only Matthew records their story. Traditionally called "wise men" or "kings," Matthew just calls them magi—a name associated with holy people who practiced astrology elsewhere in the ancient Near East. Although named in later traditions (Melchior, Caspar, Balthazar), Matthew gives them no names. In fact, even though nearly every modern depiction numbers the magi at three, Matthew does not even tell us how many they were.

For Matthew, what matters is not who the magi were but what they did: they saw Jesus' significance and set out to worship him. Though foreigners from the East, they saw more clearly than homegrown Judeans. Though not Jewish, they knew greatness where it appeared. Though at a distance, they made the trek. Though uncertain of the destination, they set out anyway—and asked for directions.

Whoever the magi were, they show us what Jesus' arrival should prompt all discerning souls to do: drop everything and go worship him.

How has worship been your response to the Christ child this season?

Prayer

O God, help us to seek Christ Jesus wherever he may be found, no matter how difficult the journey, how unclear the road, or how uncertain the timeline. Lead us, like the magi, to worship him. Amen.

Matthew 2:3-6

When King Herod heard this, he was frightened, and all Jerusalem with him; and calling together all the chief priests and scribes of the people, he inquired of them where the Messiah was to be born. They told him, "In Bethlehem of Judea; for so it has been written by the prophet:
'And you, Bethlehem, in the land of Judah,
are by no means least among the rulers of Judah;
for from you shall come a ruler
who is to shepherd my people Israel.'"

To ponder

Think of the Scriptures as the loftiest and noblest of holy things, as the richest of mines which can never be sufficiently explored. . . . Here you will find the swaddling clothes and the manger in which Christ lies. . . . Simple and lowly are these swaddling clothes, but dear is the treasure, Christ, who lies in them.—Martin Luther, "Prefaces to the Old Testament"

The gift of scripture

King Herod and all Jerusalem were frightened by the magi's news. In response, Herod asked scholars of scripture: Where is the Messiah (Christ) to be born? They quickly answered: Bethlehem. The prophet Micah had said so.

To deepen our faith, many of us look to things that seem to promise immediate spiritual mountaintop experiences: engaging worship, dynamic preachers, professional programs, celebrity devotionals, or emotionally provocative music. But we already have a goldmine close at hand: the Bible. Luther described it as "the richest of mines" and "dear is the treasure, Christ, who lies in" it. Although not always the easiest, most straightforward book to make sense of, the Bible's words of promise are foundational to creeds, spiritual writings, and sacred songs to this day.

In the Bible we encounter Christ. How might you reengage this source of life in the new year?

Prayer

O Christ, you meet us in the words of scripture. As we hear and read these words, strengthen our faith and hope in you. Amen.

January 1 / Christmas 1

Matthew 2:7-8

Then Herod secretly called for the wise men and learned from them the exact time when the star had appeared. Then he sent them to Bethlehem, saying, "Go and search diligently for the child; and when you have found him, bring me word so that I may also go and pay him homage."

To ponder

If you don't like something, change it. If you can't change it, change your attitude.—Maya Angelou, "Maya Angelou: In Her Own Words"

Embracing change, embracing gift

When change happens in our lives, we often try at all costs to stop it. When the magi report the arrival of a king, Herod plots to take him out. Like many rulers in antiquity (and today), he acts aggressively to protect his status and power. In the process, he nearly kills the Savior of the universe.

We often respond similarly when our situation is threatened, our social privilege jeopardized, or our status challenged. Someone I know once feared losing his job, although he hated it and it was hard on his health. Then one day it happened: his job was cut. And while he first despaired, the change became a door to new life that he had needed for a long time.

Changes happen in our lives, and a better model of response than Herod is Joseph. Upon hearing of Mary's pregnancy, he first intends to dissolve their engagement. But at an angel's encouragement, he chooses differently and embraces the unexpected interruption as a gift from God and source of new life—for him and for others.

Changes happen. Will we try at all costs to stop them? Or, like Joseph, will we strive to embrace the gift God may have for us in them?

Prayer

God, grant me the serenity to accept the things I cannot change, courage to change the things I can, and wisdom to know the difference. Amen. (Reinhold Niebuhr, "Serenity Prayer")

Matthew 2:9-12

When they had heard the king, they set out; and there, ahead of them, went the star that they had seen at its rising, until it stopped over the place where the child was. When they saw that the star had stopped, they were overwhelmed with joy. On entering the house, they saw the child with Mary his mother; and they knelt down and paid him homage. Then, opening their treasure chests, they offered him gifts of gold, frankincense, and myrrh. And having been warned in a dream not to return to Herod, they left for their own country by another road.

To ponder

When I stand before God at the end of my life, I would hope that I would not have a single bit of talent left and could say "I used everything you gave me." —Erma Bombeck, "The Wit and Wisdom of Erma Bombeck"

A spirituality of giving up

Life-changing spiritual experiences often require something of us. Wherever they started, the magi's journey probably required several weeks. But at their destination, they "were overwhelmed with joy." They found and worshiped the Christ child, bestowing valuable gifts as offerings.

The magi expended a great deal of time, resources, and energy in this trek. The same is true for our spirituality, at least if it is to be alive and engaged. Although God neither requires nor needs anything from us, a faith that fully receives God's gifts must be willing to change, to give things up, and to welcome a spiritual makeover by the Holy Spirit.

It was one thing for the magi to see the star and its significance. It was quite another for them to set out in response. How is God calling you to pay homage to Christ? As with the magi, responding to Christ in worship is not an armchair activity.

Prayer

O God, beckon us to give up what is unnecessary to receive and embrace what is most necessary, Christ our Lord. Amen.

January 3

Matthew 2:13-15

Now after [the magi] had left, an angel of the Lord appeared to Joseph in a dream and said, "Get up, take the child and his mother, and flee to Egypt, and remain there until I tell you; for Herod is about to search for the child, to destroy him." Then Joseph got up, took the child and his mother by night, and went to Egypt, and remained there until the death of Herod. This was to fulfill what had been spoken by the Lord through the prophet, "Out of Egypt I have called my son."

To ponder

The children of immigrants don't get to be children. We lose our innocence watching our parents' backs bend, break. I am an old soul because when I am young, I watch my parents' spirits get slaughtered.—Lenelle Moïse, "The Children of Immigrants"

Jesus the immigrant

According to Matthew, Jesus was a child immigrant. Within two years of being born, his family departed for Egypt. They left by night because they had to. They left for the same reason many immigrants do: safety. In so doing, Jesus' path paralleled that of ancient Israel, whom God brought out of Egypt.

This was probably not the way Joseph and Mary had envisioned the early years of their family.

While the historic experiences of immigrants vary, there are many commonalities: unfair stereotypes, unequal pay, limited employment opportunities, little political voice, and xenophobic hostility. The holy family presumably experienced these things, however long their stay in Egypt was.

As a child and an adult, Jesus had "nowhere to lay his head" (Matthew 8:20). He didn't have stability. He moved when his parents did. But this child did not come for stability and security. He came to know the challenges of our transitory life, so that he might save all earthly sojourners.

Prayer

Lord Jesus Christ, you crossed every border between divinity and humanity to make your home with us. Help us to welcome you in newcomers, immigrants, and refugees. Amen.

January 4

Matthew 2:16-18

When Herod saw that he had been tricked by the wise men, he was infuriated, and he sent and killed all the children in and around Bethlehem who were two years old or under, according to the time that he had learned from the wise men. Then was fulfilled what had been spoken through the prophet Jeremiah:

"A voice was heard in Ramah,

wailing and loud lamentation,

Rachel weeping for her children;

she refused to be consoled, because they are no more."

To ponder

Though I walk through the valley of the shadow of death, I shall fear no evil; for you are with me.—Psalm 23:4

When things seem at their worst

Most portrayals of biblical scenes associated with Christmas are peaceful and serene. They show humble shepherds, quiet animals, and an unfussy baby. But not all was calm and bright in the world Jesus entered.

Herod the Great ruled Judea for nearly four decades (37 to 4 BCE). He was loyal to Rome and ruthless to rivals. He prohibited protests, maintained an extensive bodyguard, and killed anyone suspicious. He had two sons strangled on treason charges. Caesar said it was "better to be Herod's pig than his son." According to the historian Josephus (in *Jewish Antiquities*), Herod feared no one would grieve his death, so he ordered the execution of distinguished guests at his funeral to ensure mourning (an order not carried out). This man was king that first Christmas. Although historians debate whether Matthew's story happened as told, it fits Herod's character.

If you think our world today is worse off than ever, think again. The world Jesus entered was a scary place, with violent rulers and lots of suffering. That's the world Jesus came to save.

If you think this world is beyond hope, you're wrong. If you think your world is too broken for redemption, God disagrees. Jesus arrived in the shadow of violence to save us all.

When the world is at its worst, Christ appears.

Prayer

O Christ Jesus, come among us today to redeem, renew, restore, and reign. Amen.

January 5

Matthew 2:19-21

When Herod died, an angel of the Lord suddenly appeared in a dream to Joseph in Egypt and said, "Get up, take the child and his mother, and go to the land of Israel, for those who were seeking the child's life are dead." Then Joseph got up, took the child and his mother, and went to the land of Israel.

To ponder

I will make a way in the wilderness and rivers in the desert.
—Isaiah 43:19

A way through the fog

Many of us want a map for our life of faith. We want to know where our journey leads, its significant landmarks, and how long it will last. We want to know so that we are not surprised.

But the life of faith isn't like that. Take Joseph, for example. Without clear forewarning, the Lord guides Joseph three times—by an angel or dream—to relocate. As far as we know, Joseph did not anticipate these transitions. He simply responded when prompted.

The life of faith is like that: moments of clarity in a land otherwise filled with guesswork. At junctures, we sense God's leading. At other times, we carry on as faithfully as we can.

On our wedding night, my wife and I were driving along Lake Superior when dense fog rolled in. We suddenly could not see more than ten feet ahead. I stopped at a gas station, uncertain we could continue. I did not want our honeymoon to start with disaster. Suddenly, a truck came—and it had excellent fog lights. I pulled behind and followed, all the way to our destination. The truck became for us a guiding angel on an otherwise impassable path.

Sometimes the journey of faith feels like a slog through dense fog. But God does not abandon us. Precisely when needed, by means sometimes surprising, God in Christ provides a way.

Prayer

Guide me ever, great Redeemer, pilgrim through this barren land; I am weak, but you are mighty; hold me with your pow'rful hand. Amen. ("Guide me ever, great Redeemer," ELW 618)

Matthew 2:22-23

But when [Joseph] heard that Archelaus was ruling over Judea in place of his father Herod, he was afraid to go there. And after being warned in a dream, he went away to the district of Galilee. There he made his home in a town called Nazareth, so that what had been spoken through the prophets might be fulfilled, "He will be called a Nazorean."

To ponder

God is forming us into a new people. And the place of that formation is in the small moments of today.—Tish Harrison Warren, *Liturgy of the Ordinary*

God's handiwork in the random

At first glance, the many relocations of Jesus' family seem random. They emigrate to Egypt to avoid a ruler, return after he dies, then relocate to avoid another. The early years of Jesus' life were hardly stable and safe.

But God works through the seemingly random events of life. Four times in chapter two, Matthew points out how events of Jesus' life fulfill scripture (see verses 6, 15, 18, 23). Random as they may seem, God uses such aspects of our lives to shape us, bless others, and make us who we are.

Upon starting the ministry role I now occupy, I told a friend: "It feels like a bunch of puzzle pieces in my life suddenly fell into place." I didn't see it coming. But at that moment, God's handiwork throughout my life was clear.

My daughter uses a rainbow loom to make rubber band bracelets. Their beauty lies in how they interweave different colors into a magnificent pattern. That's what God does with the scattered pieces of our lives.

How is God at work through the random events of your life?

Prayer

O God, weave the scattered pieces of our lives into a beautiful tapestry of grace, through Christ our Lord. Amen.

Household Blessings and Prayers

An evening service of light for Advent

This brief order may be used on any evening during the season of Advent. If the household has an Advent wreath (one candle for each of the four weeks of Advent), it may be lighted during this service. Alternatively, one simple candle (perhaps a votive candle) may be lighted instead.

Lighting the Advent wreath

May this candle/these candles be a sign of the coming light of Christ.

One or more candles may be lighted.

Week 1: Lighting the first candle
Blessed are you, God of Jacob, for you promise to transform

weapons of war into implements of planting and harvest and to teach us your way of peace; you promise that our night of sin is far gone and that your day of salvation is dawning.

As we light the first Advent candle, wake us from our sleep, wrap us in your light, empower us to live honorably, and guide us along your path of peace.

O house of Jacob, come,
let us walk in the light of the Lord. Amen.

Week 2: Lighting the first two candles
Blessed are you, God of hope, for you promise to bring forth a shoot from the stump of Jesse who will bring justice to the poor, who will deliver the needy and crush the oppressor, who will stand as a signal of hope for all people.

As we light these candles, turn our wills to bear the fruit of repentance, transform our hearts to live in justice and harmony with one another, and fix our eyes on the shoot from Jesse, Jesus Christ, the hope of all nations.

O people of hope, come,
let us rejoice in the faithfulness of the Lord. Amen.

Week 3: Lighting three candles
Blessed are you, God of might and majesty, for you promise to make the desert rejoice and blossom, to watch over the strangers, and to set the prisoners free.

As we light these candles, satisfy our hunger with your good gifts, open our eyes to the great things you have done for us, and fill us with patience until the coming of the Lord Jesus.

O ransomed people of the Lord, come,
let us travel on God's holy way
and enter into Zion with singing. Amen.

Week 4: Lighting all four candles
Blessed are you, God of hosts, for you promised to send a Son, Emmanuel, who brought your presence among us; and you promise through your Son Jesus to save us from our sin.

As we light these candles, turn again to us in mercy; strengthen our faith in the word spoken by your prophets; restore us and give us life that we may be saved.

O house of David, come,
let us rejoice, for the Son of God, Emmanuel,
comes to be with us. Amen.

Reading
Read the scripture passage printed in the devotion for the day.

Hymn
One of the following hymns may be sung. The hymn might be accompanied by small finger cymbals.

"Light one candle to watch for Messiah," ELW 240
"People, look east," ELW 248
"Savior of the nations, come," ELW 263

During the final seven days of the Advent season (beginning on December 17), the hymn "O come, O come, Emmanuel" (ELW 257) is particularly appropriate. The stanzas of that hymn are also referred to as the "O Antiphons." The first stanza of the hymn could be sung each day during the final days before Christmas in addition to the stanza that is specifically appointed for the day.

Table prayer for Advent

Blessed are you, O Lord our God,
the one who is, who was, and who is to come.
At this table you fill us with good things.
May these gifts strengthen us
to share with the hungry and all those in need,
as we wait and watch for your coming among us
in Jesus Christ our Lord. Amen.

Lighting the Christmas tree

Use this prayer when you first illumine the tree or when you gather at the tree.

Holy God,
we praise you as we light this tree.
It gives light to this place
as you shine light into darkness through Jesus,
the light of the world.

God of all,
we thank you for your love,
the love that has come to us in Jesus.
Be with us now as we remember that gift of love,
and help us to share that love with a yearning world.

Creator God,
you made the stars in the heavens.
Thank you for the light that shines on us in Jesus,
the bright morning star.
Amen.

Blessing of the nativity scene

This blessing may be used when figures are added to the nativity scene and throughout the days of Christmas.

Bless us, O God, as we remember a humble birth. With each angel and shepherd we place here before you, show us the wonder found in a stable. In song and prayer, silence and awe, we adore your gift of love, Christ Jesus our Savior. Amen.

Table prayer for the twelve days of Christmas (December 25–January 5)

With joy and gladness we feast upon your love, O God.
You have come among us in Jesus, your Son,
and your presence now graces this table.
May Christ dwell in us
that we might bear his love to all the world,
for he is Lord forever and ever. Amen.

Blessing for a home at Epiphany

Matthew writes that when the magi saw the shining star stop overhead, they were filled with joy. "On entering the house, they saw the child with Mary his mother" (Matthew 2:11). In the home, Christ is met in family and friends, in visitors and strangers. In the home, faith is shared, nurtured, and put into action. In the home, Christ is welcome.

Twelfth Night (January 5), Epiphany of Our Lord (January 6), or another day during the time after Epiphany offers an occasion for gathering with friends and family members for a blessing of the home. Someone may lead the greeting and blessing, while another person may read the scripture passage. Following an Eastern European tradition, a visual blessing may be inscribed with white chalk above the main door; for example, 20 + CMB + 23. The numbers change with each new year. The three letters stand for either the ancient Latin blessing Christe mansionem benedicat, *which means "Christ, bless this house," or the legendary names of the magi (Caspar, Melchior, and Balthasar).*

Greeting

Peace to this house and to all who enter here.
By wisdom a house is built,
and through understanding it is established;
through knowledge its rooms are filled
with rare and beautiful treasures. (*Prov. 24:3-4*)

Reading

As we prepare to ask God's blessing on this household,
let us listen to the words of scripture.
In the beginning was the Word,
and the Word was with God, and the Word was God.
He was in the beginning with God.
All things came into being through him,
and without him not one thing came into being.
What has come into being in him was life,
and the life was the light of all people.
The Word became flesh and lived among us, and we have seen
    his glory,
the glory as of a father's only son, full of grace and truth.
From his fullness we have all received, grace upon grace.
(*John 1:1-4, 14, 16*)

Inscription

This inscription may be made with chalk above the entrance:

20 + C M B + 23

Write the appropriate character (left) while speaking the text (right).

The magi of old, known as

C   Caspar,

M   Melchior, and

B   Balthasar,

followed the star of God's Son who came to dwell among us

20   two thousand

23   and twenty-three years ago.

+   Christ, bless this house,

+   and remain with us throughout the new year.

Prayer of Blessing

O God,

you revealed your Son to all people by the shining light of a star.

We pray that you bless this home and all who live here with your gracious presence.

May your love be our inspiration, your wisdom our guide, your truth our light, and your peace our benediction; through Christ our Lord. Amen.

Then everyone may walk from room to room, blessing the house with incense or by sprinkling with water, perhaps using a branch from the Christmas tree.

Table prayer for Epiphany

Generous God,
you have made yourself known in Jesus, the light of the world.
As this food and drink give us refreshment,
so strengthen us by your spirit,
that as your baptized sons and daughters
we may share your light with all the world.
Grant this through Christ our Lord.
Amen.